We

Hope this

Love Robert + Melissa ♡

2016

MW00698341

The future's
this way.⟶

Published by Sourcebooks, Inc.
P.O. Box 4410, Naperville, Illinois 60567-4410
(630) 961-3900
Fax: (630) 961-2168
www.sourcebooks.com

Originally published in 2013 in the United Kingdom by Bantam Press, an imprint of Transworld Publishers.

Printed and bound in China.

LEO 10 9 8 7 6 5 4 3 2 1

If you can't remember what it says on the cover, give up now.

Waldo Pancake

 sourcebooks

You know everything I ever said to you? I was pretty much making it all up on the spot.

Now go do the same.

The only thing that keeps me going is how brilliant and amazing I am.

The early bird gets the worm.

The bird with worms in its fridge also gets the worm, minus all the hassle of having to wake up early.

·break the rules

TRAVEL

QUICK, BEFORE
FLYING BECOMES
ENVIRONMENTALLY
UNTENABLE.

If someone's had more
hot meals than you've
done some other completely
unrelated action, be sure
to listen to them carefully.

Recycle.
Or the world
gets it.

Sometimes it's
← ———— better to say
nothing at all.

↑

Wish I hadn't
said that.

↑

And that.

YOU ARE BRILLIANT

if you choose this page.

YOU ARE
AN IDIOT

if you choose this one.

When life gives
you lemons, make
lemonade.

Then start
selling it.

But not before you've used a break-even analysis to determine if your idea can really make money. Maybe write a business plan, including a profit/loss forecast and a cash-flow analysis.

Lemons. Don't jump in.

You know how people say,
"I'll sleep when I'm dead"?
They won't. You have to be
alive to go to sleep.

IGNORE ALL ADVICE.

Even if it has a drop shadow.

Today is the tomorrow you worried about yesterday.

Tomorrow is you rolling your eyes for wasting yesterday reading this crap.

Remember: you can always be a bum.

You're one ~~in a million.~~
of 7 billion

Keep turning
the pages.
Of your life.

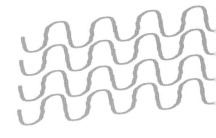

Push the envelope.
With your résumé inside.
Through the door of
prospective employers.

Don't go bald.

But if you do, own it.

But don't.

But if you do, own it.

Don't though.

On throwing your mortarboard in the air:

Attach a reel of cotton to one corner for ease of retrieval.

I know it sounds bad,
but being a psychopath
might actually help,
career-wise.

Be the first in the pool.

Then get out when everyone else gets in.

Become the world record
holder for long fingernails.*

*You won't be able to use touch screens though.

Don't fall for the carrot and stick.

Just go buy a carrot for hardly any money then pick up a stick from the ground for free.

Hold your mug
the way bosses
do in films.*

*Firm grip, close to body.

EMBRACE CHANGE.

Unless Change is the name of the person interviewing you.

←——— UNLESS the job you're going for is chief hugger.

Learn something new every day.

You'll probably have to forget something to make room though.

Career:

to move swiftly and in an uncontrolled way.

What I'm saying is,
don't let people know
what a genius you are.

———————→

Nobody
likes a
know-it-all.

Love the skin you're in.
Before it goes all old
and wrinkly.

Listen to others...

if only to feel better about yourself.

Nobody accomplished anything amazing all by themselves.

Apart from me with this book.

Don't jiggle your knee.

It's really annoying.

Smell stuff.

Stuff. Smell it.

READ MORE.

↑
Like this for example.

Drugs aren't cool.

You think you're so it with your cod liver oil and vitamin C, but nobody's impressed.

Live, believe, worry a bit.

Sometimes having a good personality just means you're really loud and annoying.

Advice for when you get famous:

Have you seen those signatures that look like a bit of squiggly pubic hair? Design yours that way. That way, you'll never need to carry a pen. Just pull off a pube and glue it down whenever your autograph is requested. You will need to carry a glue stick, by the way.

Don't tell people you shave
your whole face, leaving
just the eyebrow bits.

Be polite.

But not too polite. For example, say "gesundheit" when someone sneezes. Then inform said sneezer that was their one and only gesundheit from you. Every time they sneeze after that, give them your "we've discussed this" face.

(Make yourself heard.)

Don't be a show-off.

Frown more. Makes a change from all the fake smiles.

DON'T JOG.

I've been looking at the people who do, and it seems to be making them fat.

Walk under ladders.
That way, when it
all goes wrong you'll
have something to blame.

GO OUT-DOORS.

It makes coming back in so much better.

Adults must be accompanied by a sense of impending

DOOM.

Sliced bread isn't as amazing as everyone says.

STOP READING THIS STUPID BOOK AND GET ON WITH YOUR LIFE.

Ignore the small print.

Er, I said ignore it?

Stay until the
credits end.